A Green Fig Book

Illustrated & Designed by

CHY Illustration & Design

Name:

NOTE TO PARENTS & EDUCATORS

Where are They? is another book by Green Fig elucidating a fundamental in the Muslim creed that God exists without a place. Before creating the place, God existed without a place; and after He created the place, God exists without a place. God does not change and does not need anything.

In the book al-'Akd al-Farīd authored by Aḥmad the son of Muḥammad the Andalusian (Died 328 H) it is stated: "And 'Aliyy was asked: "Where was our Lord before He created the heaven and earth?" So he said: Where necessitates the place and God existed eternally without a place." It is important to teach kids that God is not like His creation, and is not attributed with a place, hence it is contrary to the religion to ask "Where is God?".

Where are They? is written using animals' homes, a theme that children love and is artfully illustrated.

We love to hear from you at: info@greenfigbooks.com.

Green Fig Staff

Where is Dan?
Dan is at school.
Sitting at his desk.

**The lesson today is about
animal homes.**

ANIMAL HOMES
EAGLE
ROOSTER
SQUIRREL
BEAVER
COW
SHEEP
SPIDER
HYENA
ANT

Where is the ant?
In the ant hill.

Where is the cow?
In the barn.

Where is the sheep?
In the fold.

Where is the rooster?
In its coop.

Where is the hyena?
In its den.

Where is the squirrel?
In its drey.

Where is the spider?
In its web.

Where is the beaver?
In its lodge.

Where is the eagle?
In its eyrie.

WE USE "**WHERE?**"
TO ASK ABOUT A PLACE.

ONE MUST NOT ASK "WHERE IS GOD?",
BECAUSE GOD IS NOT IN A PLACE.

GOD IS NOT ON EARTH.
GOD IS NOT IN THE HEAVENS.

GOD IS NOT IN ANY PLACE.

Where do humans and animals live?

On earth.

Where do angels live?

In the heavens.

Activity

More Animal Homes:

1- Where does a horse live ? ___________________________

2- Where does a bee live ? ___________________________

3- Where does a lion live ? ___________________________

4- Where does a rabbit live ? ___________________________

5- Where does a snail live ? ___________________________

Connect the animals with their homes:

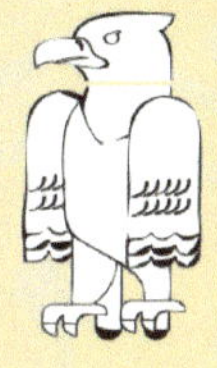 **Eagle**

 **Lodge**

 **Squirrel**

 **Coop**

 **Rooster**

 **Web**

 **Beaver**

 **Eyrie**

 **Spider**

 **Drey**

Encourage your child to memorize:

Imām ʿAliyy said,

أين سؤال عن المكان وكان الله ولا مكان ولا زمان وهو الان على ما عليه كان

Which means:
"Where is a question about the place, and God existed eternally
without a place and without time and He is now as He was."

Narrated by Imām an-Nasafiyy (438-508 A.H.) in his book Bahrul Kalām

The Proud Muslim Kids series by Green Fig is designed to engagingly teach youngsters basic concepts of Islam in a way that speaks to their hearts and minds. Each book in the series is crafted by a staff of qualified educators, writers, illustrators, parents and children. Not only is the Proud Muslim Kids series designed to supplement the early childhood and elementary Islamic curriculum, it is a great addition to any school or home library. Covering a wide variety of topics such as the Five Pillars of Islam, Islamic culture, and Islamic history, parents and children will return to these books and enjoy them together time and time again.

Green Fig